THE FABULOUS LOST & FOUND

AND THE LITTLE CHINESE MOUSE

WRITTEN BY MARK PALLIS
ILLUSTRATED BY PETER BAYNTON

NEU WESTEND
— PRESS —

Thanks Luther and Taxian - MP

For Hannah and Skye - PB

First Printing, 2020
ISBN: 978-1-913595-31-9
NeuWestendPress.com

THE FABULOUS LOST & FOUND

FOUND

AND THE LITTLE CHINESE MOUSE

WRITTEN BY MARK PALLIS

ILLUSTRATED BY PETER BAYNTON

NEU WESTEND
— PRESS —

In the middle of the big city is a tiny
yellow building. If anyone loses anything, this is
where it ends up.

It is called the Lost and Found.

Mr and Mrs Frog keep everything safe, hoping that someday every lost watch and bag and phone and toy and shoe and cheesegrater will find its owner again.

But the shop is very small. And there are so many lost things. It is all quite a squeeze, but still, it's fabulous.

One sunny day, a little mouse walked in.

"Welcome," said Mrs Frog. "What have you lost?"

wǒ bǎ wǒ de mào zi nòng diū le
"我把我的帽子弄丢了。" said the mouse.

Mr and Mrs Frog could not speak Chinese. They had no idea what the little mouse was saying.

What shall we do? they wondered.

Maybe she's lost an umbrella. Everyone loses an umbrella at least twice, thought Mr Frog.

"Have you lost this?" asked Mr Frog.

shì yì bǎ yǔ sǎn ma? bú shì
"是一把雨伞吗? 不是。" replied the
mouse.

Then Mrs Frog remembered something that
had been handed in a few months ago...

"Is this yours?" Mrs Frog asked, holding up a chunk of cheese.

shì zhī shì ma? bú shì。 zhī shì huì fā chòu !
"是芝士吗? 不是。芝士会发臭！" said the mouse.

"Time to put that cheese in the bin dear," said Mr Frog.

"Maybe the word '帽子' means coat," said Mr Frog.
(mào zi)

"Now where did I put that nice

yellow one?"

"Got it!" said Mr Frog.

yí jiàn wài tào ma? bú shì。wǒ nòng diū le wǒ de mào zi。
"一件外套吗? 不是。我弄丢了我的帽子。"
said the mouse.

She was starting to feel a bit frustrated.

"We need to keep trying," said Mrs Frog.

bú shì yì tiáo wéi jīn
不是一条围巾 。

bú shì yí tiáo kù zi
不是一条裤子。

bú shì yí jiàn máo yī
不是一件毛衣。

bú shì yì shuāng xié
不是一双鞋。

bú shì yí fù tài yáng yǎn jìng
不是一副太阳眼镜。

wǒ bǎ wǒ de mào zi nòng diū le
"我把我的帽子弄丢了。"

said the mouse.

bú shì liǎng liàng zì xíng chē
不是两辆自行车。

bú shì yì tái diàn nǎo
不是一台电脑。

bú shì sān běn shū
不是三本书。

bú shì sì gēn xiāng jiāo
不是四根香蕉。

bú shì wǔ bǎ yào shi
不是五把钥匙。

It was no good. A fat wet tear rolled
down the mouse's cheek.

"How about a nice cup of tea?" asked Mrs Frog kindly.

wǒ xǐ huān chá, xiè xie
"我喜欢茶，谢谢。" replied the mouse. They sat together,

sipping their tea and all feeling a bit sad.

Suddenly, the mouse realised she could try pointing.

She pointed at her head.

mào zi
"帽子" she said.

"I've got it!" exclaimed Mrs Frog, leaping up.

"A wig of course!" said Mrs Frog.

bú shì yì dǐng jiǎ fà
"不是一顶假发。" said the mouse.

bú shì hóng sè de
不是红色的。

bú shì jīn sè de
不是金色的。

bú shì zōng sè de
不是棕色的。

bú shì cǎi sè de
不是彩色的。

bú shì lǜ sè de
不是绿色的。

"What about this?"
asked Mr Frog, pulling back
a curtain.

mào zi
"帽子" exclaimed the
mouse.

mào zi
"Ah, so ' 帽子' means hat.
Wonderful!" Mr and Mrs
Frog cheered.

tài gāo le
太高了。

tài xiǎo le
太小了。

tài jǐn le
太紧了。

tài dà le
太大了。

"One hat left," said Mrs Frog, reaching all the way to the back of the cupboard.

"It couldn't be this old thing, could it?"

wǒ de mào zi
我的帽子。

wǒ zhǎo dào wǒ de mào zi le
我找到我的帽子了！

fēi cháng xiè xie nǐ
非常谢谢你。," said the mouse.

And just like that, the mouse found her hat.

zài jiàn
"再见。" she said, as she skipped away.

zài jiàn
"再见。" replied Mr and Mrs Frog.

"I wonder who will come tomorrow?" said Mr Frog.
Mrs Frog put her arm around him.

"I don't know," she replied, giving him a squeeze,
"but whoever it is, we'll do our best to help."

LEARNING TO LOVE LANGUAGES

An additional language opens a child's mind, broadens their horizons and enriches their emotional life. Research has shown that the time between a child's birth and their sixth or seventh birthday is a "golden period" when they are most receptive to new languages. This is because they have an in-built ability to distinguish the sounds they hear and make sense of them. The Story-powered Language Learning Method taps into these natural abilities.

HOW THE STORY-POWERED LANGUAGE LEARNING METHOD WORKS

We create an emotionally engaging and funny story for children and adults to enjoy together, just like any other picture book. Studies show that social interaction, like enjoying a book together, is critical in language learning.

Through the story, we introduce a relatable character who speaks only in the new language. This helps build empathy and a positive attitude towards people who speak different languages. These are both important aspects in laying the foundations for lasting language acquisition in a child's life.

As the story progresses, the child naturally works with the characters to discover the meanings of a wide range of fun new words. Strategic use of humour ensures that this subconscious learning is rewarded with laughter; the child feels good and the first seeds of a lifelong love of languages are sown.

For more information and free downloads visit www.neuwestendpress.com

ALL THE BEAUTIFUL CHINESE WORDS AND PHRASES FROM OUR STORY

wǒ nòng diū le wǒ de mào zi	I've lost my hat
yì bǎ yǔ sǎn	umbrella
zhī shì	cheese
ta huì fā chòu	it stinks
wài tào	coat
wéi jīn	scarf
kù zi	trousers
tài yáng yǎn jìng	sunglasses
máo yī	sweater
xié zi	shoes
yī	one
èr; liǎng	two
sān	three
sì	four
wǔ	five
diàn nǎo	computer
shū	book
yào shi	key
xiāng jiāo	banana
zì xíng chē	bicycle
wǒ xǐ huān chá	I love tea
xiè xie nǐ	thank you
jiǎ fà	wig
hóng sè	red
jīn sè; jīn fà	blond

zōng sè、hè sè	brown
lǜ sè	green
cǎi sè、duō sè de	multicoloured
bú shì	no
wǒ de mào zi	my hat
tài gāo	too tall
tài dà	too big
tài xiǎo	too small
tài jǐn	too tight
wǒ zhǎo dào wǒ de mào zi le	I've found my hat
fēi cháng xiè xie nǐ	thank you very much
zài jiàn	goodbye

Pronunciation Tips

ū 1st tone. Keep voice high and even.
é 2nd tone. Voice rises, like asking a question.
ǒ 3rd tone. Voice falls then rises, like a dip.
è 4th tone. Voice high then drops quickly.

x = similar to 'sh' in sheep.
q = similar to 'ch' in cheap
c = similar to 'ts' in its
zh = similar to 'j' in jam
ao = similar to 'ou' in loud
ou = similar to 'oa' in boat

THE WORLD OF
THE FABULOUS LOST & FOUND

THIS STORY IS ALSO AVAILABLE IN...

FRENCH

SPANISH

ITALIAN   CZECH

WELSH

KOREAN   GERMAN   HEBREW

SWEDISH   POLISH   SLOVAKIAN

VIETNAMESE   LATIN   PORTUGUESE

...AND MANY MORE LANGUAGES!

ENJOYED IT?
WRITE A REVIEW AND
LET US KNOW!

@MARK_PALLIS ON TWITTER
WWW.MARKPALLIS.COM

@PETERBAYNTON ON INSTAGRAM
WWW.PETERBAYNTON.COM

Made in the USA
Las Vegas, NV
15 November 2022

59496875R00024